DATE DUE		

Firefighter Tom to the Rescue!

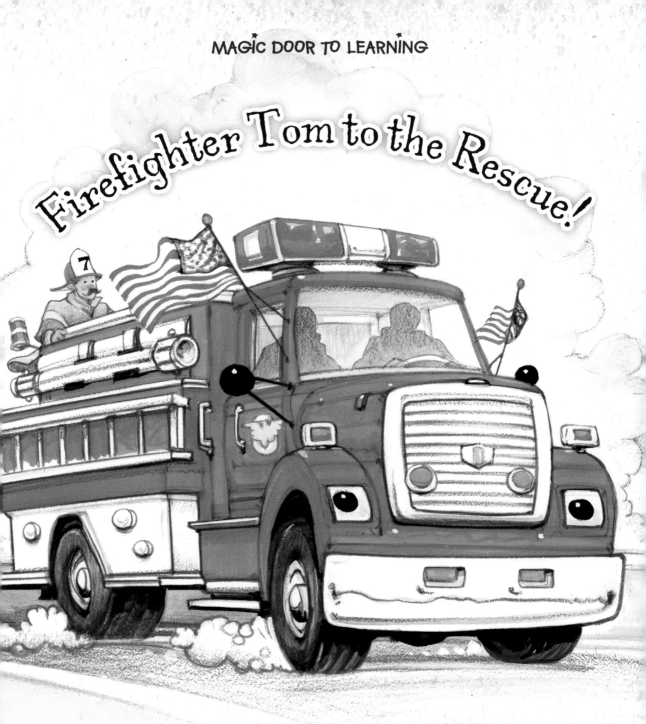

Written by Charnan Simon • Illustrated by Joel Snyder

The Child's World

Published in the United States of America by The Child's World®
PO Box 326 • Chanhassen, MN 55317-0326
800-599-READ • www.childsworld.com

Reading Adviser

Cecilia Minden-Cupp, PhD, Former Language and Literacy Program Director,
Harvard Graduate School of Education, Cambridge, Massachusetts

Acknowledgments

The Child's World®: Mary Berendes, Publishing Director

Editorial Directions, Inc.: E. Russell Primm, Editorial Director and Project Manager;
Katie Marsico, Associate Editor; Judith Shiffer, Assistant Editor; Caroline Wood, Editorial Assistant

The Design Lab: Kathleen Petelinsek, Design and Art Production

Library of Congress Cataloging-in-Publication Data

Simon, Charnan.
  Firefighter Tom to the rescue! / written by Charnan Simon; illustrated by Joel Snyder.
    p. cm. — (Magic door to learning)
  ISBN: 1-59296-621-7 (library bound : alk. paper)
  1. Fire extinction—Juvenile literature. 2. Fire fighters—Juvenile literature.
I. Snyder, Joel. II. Title. III. Series.
TH9148.S537 2006
628.9'25—dc22   2006001412

A book is a door, a magic door.
It can take you places
you have never been before.
Ready? Set?
Turn the page.
Open the door.
Now it is time to explore.

Firefighter Tom is an important guy. When he is on the job, he eats and sleeps at the fire station.

He makes sure the fire engines
are always ready to go.

8

He keeps his equipment
in perfect working order!

Firefighter Tom doesn't just fight fires. Sometimes he rescues people who are stuck in an elevator or swimmers who need help getting out of the water.

Firefighter Tom makes sure all the
fire hydrants in the city work.
He teaches people about fire safety.

13

14

The alarm goes off!
Firefighter Tom jumps into action!

Firefighter Tom turns the siren
up as loud as it can go as he
races to the fire.

EEEE

EEEEE!!

Hissssssss! The water from
the hose puts out the flames.

19

Whewwww! Firefighter Tom
rescues a mom and her baby.

Firefighter Tom is
an important guy!

Our story is over, but there is still much to explore beyond the magic door!

Did you know that you can help fight fires, too? Sit down with your family and talk about what you would do if your house caught on fire. What would be the best ways to get out of your home? Where would you meet outside your house? You might even practice how you would escape from your home if there was a fire. See how long it takes everyone to get outside safely. Being prepared is the best way to help fight fires!

These books will help you explore at the library and at home:

Cousins, Lucy. *Maisy's Fire Engine*. Cambridge, Mass.: Candlewick Press, 2002.

Demarest, Chris L. *Firefighters A to Z*. New York: Margaret K. McElderry
    Books, 2000.

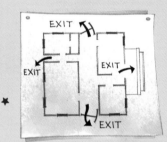

About the Author

Charnan Simon lives in Madison, Wisconsin, where she can usually be found sitting at her desk and writing books, unless she is sitting at her desk and looking out the window. Charnan has one husband, two daughters, and two very helpful cats.

About the Illustrator

Joel Snyder, a graduate of the Rhode Island School of Design, has illustrated books, magazines, and various other publications (most of which have been for children). He lives in Little Falls, New York, with his youngest son.

24